Artist's Cover: Madelynn Gingold, *Bleached Brancusi*, 2018 (after Constantin Brancusi, *The Kiss*, 1916).

For the History Boy

Printed in NYC.

Samizdat Press

ISBN-13: 978-0-692-19241-2

1-6944102311

United States Copyright Office

The Safety of The State:
America v. Trump/Putin

By Madelynn Gingold

Table of Contents

"When you see a rattlesnake poised to strike, you do not wait until he has struck to crush him."

Franklin D. Roosevelt

"Experience teaches us that it is much easier to prevent an enemy from posting themselves than it is to dislodge them after they have got possession."

George Washington

"I am a firm believer in the people. If given the truth they can be depended upon to meet any national crisis. The great point is to bring them the real facts."

Abraham Lincoln

"It may not be good for America, but it's damn good for CBS."
"The money's rolling in and this is fun."

Les Moonves, CBS Chair

THE TIME HAS COME, 2017

"The time has come," the Walrus said,
"Here's the only thing.
Whose country is it, anyway
And who's in the West Wing?"

"But wait a bit," replied the R's,
"Before we have our chat;
For some of us are out of breath,
And all of us got fat!"
"No hurry," said the Mainstream Press.
They thanked them much for that.

"We weep for you."
Now they say,
"We deeply sympathize.
With sobs and tears we're sorting out
Corruption and Big Lies."

"You can't blame us,
The Mainstream Press
So sorry it's too late
We didn't print the dossier
Before November 8."

"Although we knew, before that date,
That bad things had been done,
The hacking, then the SABOTAGE,
We could not spoil the fun."

"Americans!" declare the R's,
"You've had a pleasant run
It's Putin's turn to rule you now
Your democracy is done."
(Okay, not all. But almost every one.)

The heads of those with Russian ties
Are what we chiefly need
Plated, salted.
Or on a pike.
So very good indeed.

"Will he become my new best friend?"

Trump

A MESSAGE FROM THE WHITE HOUSE

"We're anti-US anarchists
A kleptocratic band
We'll turn on our supporters now
The populace be damned."

"We hate the press and immigrants
Your so-called rights and laws
We're anti-Constitutional
What Emoluments Clause?"

"It's certain Jesus hates us
For the meanness that we've fanned
This chaos we create each day
It's for the Motherland!"

Such a grotesque swindle
The sabotage well timed
No game plan to undo the coup?
Does anybody mind?

WE HOLD THESE TRUTHS TO BE SELF-EVIDENT

A PRINCE WHOSE CHARACTER IS THUS MARKED BY EVERY ACT WHICH MAY DEFINE A **TYRANT,** immorality, bigotry, mendacity, trickery, ignorance, piggishness, lawlessness, bellicosity, and greed, IS UNFIT TO BE THE RULER OF A FREE PEOPLE.

We are not DISPOSED TO SUFFER … WHEN A LONG TRAIN OF ABUSES AND USURPATIONS … EVINCES A DESIGN TO REDUCE our nation UNDER ABSOLUTE DESPOTISM.

He has greatly abused power aided by THE MERCILESS Republicans WHOSE KNOWN RULE OF WARFARE IS AN UNDISTINGUISHED DESTRUCTION OF ALL norms and values that make us great and make us good.

He has OBSTRUCTED THE
ADMINISTRATION OF JUSTICE
openly and often.

He has ATTACKED our judicial
system, and our national security and
intelligence services, in an effort to
nullify truth and protect himself.

He has absolved himself from all allegiance
to his oath of office and to the
Constitution, with the goal of
ESTABLISHING ... AN ARBITRARY
GOVERNMENT ... INTRODUCING
THE SAME ABSOLUTE RULE INTO
THESE ... States as in the autocracies he
so admires.

He has EXCITED DOMESTIC
INSURRECTION AMONGST US at
Charlottesville, and domestic
CONVULSIONS everywhere he can.

He has lied ceaselessly and repeated his lies FOR THE SOLE PURPOSE OF FATIGUING the people and the press, distracting us away from his abuse of power and corruption.

He has colluded in public and private, as have his associates, family members and his officials … WAGING WAR AGAINST US.

He has… subjected … US TO A JURISDICTION FOREIGN TO OUR CONSTITUTION, on foreign soil, at Helsinki, and in the White House itself, joking and smiling, disporting himself, among hostile foreign officials, GIVING… away high state secrets and … HIS ASSENT TO THEIR ACTS … and favored policies. Gutting the State Department, undermining U.S. global power, is proof of his allegiance to an enemy state.

He has subverted our efforts to punish our
enemies, making friends with
other autocrats and forces known to be
hostile to us.

He has insulted our friends everywhere, the
NATO countries, Canada and Mexico, and
other innocent nations.

He has upended established alliances and
agreements, The Paris Climate Accords,
The Iran Nuclear Agreement and
menaced The NATO Alliance.
He has threatened …
CUTTING OFF OUR TRADE …
through tariff wars.

He has FORBIDDEN HIS GOVERNORS
TO PASS LAWS OF IMMEDIATE AND
PRESSING IMPORTANCE… THE STATE
REMAINING IN THE MEAN TIME
EXPOSED TO ALL THE DANGERS OF

INVASION FROM … foreign powers by refusing to secure the integrity of the vote. He has COMBINED WITH OTHERS, who are hostile to democracy and equal rights, to revoke THE RIGHT OF THE PEOPLE to fair representation through intimidation, voter suppression, severe reduction in the number of polling places, purging legitimate voters from the rolls and gerrymandering.

He has, with Congressional Republicans, BEEN DEPRIVING US IN MANY CASES OF THE BENEFIT OF … taxes owed to us, impoverishing the common wealth, with trillion-dollar yearly deficits, by looting the resources of the state, radically reducing just taxes on the uppermost wealthy individuals and corporations, thereby favoring the enrichment of members of his family, his Administration and its sponsors.

He has REFUSED HIS ASSENT TO LAWS, THE MOST WHOLESOME AND

NECESSARY FOR THE PUBLIC GOOD ...
Those he has appointed to head agencies for
environmental, equal rights, consumer and
financial protections, are plundering those
agencies. The Departments of Education,
Veterans Affairs, The Bureau of Land
Management, The Federal Bureau of Prisons
and others are regarded as revenue sources for
his co-looters.

He has ... collaborated with other
Republicans ... DECLARING
THEMSELVES INVESTED WITH
POWER TO LEGISLATE FOR US IN ALL
CASES WHATSOEVER, even imposing
their oppressive religious beliefs on all citizens
alike, abrogating the principle of separation of
church and state upon which our nation was
founded.

He has been stacking the courts with extreme
Right-wing judges ... TO EXTEND AN
UNWARRANTABLE JURISDICTION
OVER US ... far into the future. He and the

co-looting Republicans aim to destroy judicial precedent regarding equal rights for minorities, voting rights, reproductive rights, immigrants rights, union rights, environmental protections, consumer protections, protections against predatory loans and financial products, illegal home evictions and foreclosures, abusive student loans, and limiting bankruptcy relief for ordinary citizens.

He has UTTERLY NEGLECTED TO … protect our land and seas. He is opening our treasured national parks to drilling and pipelines and commercial exploitations, exposing our fisheries and coastlines to irreversible environmental perils.

He has ENDEAVORED TO PREVENT THE LAWS FOR NATURLIZATION OF FOREIGNERS, capriciously deporting many innocent people who have lived here for decades with their American spouses and children, including decorated members of the Armed Forces.

He has broken our laws and international treaties regarding those legally seeking asylum, fleeing for their dear lives.

He has SENT … SWARMS OF OFFICERS TO imprison children and separate them from their parents … CIRCUMSTANCES MARKED WITH CRUELTY AND PERFIDY, SCARCELY PARALLELED IN THE MOST BARBAROUS AGES, AND TOTALLY UNWORTHY OF THE HEAD OF A CIVILIZED NATION.

He has ABDICATED GOVERNMENT HERE, BY DECLARING US OUT OF HIS PROTECTION, those most vulnerable, the sick, the poor, the minorities, the youngest and the oldest.

He has ENDEAVORED, in league with other anti-American individuals and entities, to erode trust in government, respect for a free press, and support for free and mandatory public education, endangering the foundations of our democracy.

He has, with those willing to collude, been ABOLISHING OUR MOST VALUABLE LAWS AND PROTECTIONS against a system of oligarchy foreign to us.

We are scarce protected from ... HIS INVASIONS ON THE RIGHTS OF THE PEOPLE to decent wages, pensions, healthcare, and access to clean air, water and unpolluted land.

He has made clear his purpose ... ALTERING FUNDAMENTALLY THE FORMS OF OUR GOVERNMENT ... ALL HAVING IN DIRECT OBJECT THE ESTABLISHMENT OF AN

ABSOLUTE TYRANNY OVER THESE
STATES.

He has ENDEAVORED to destroy, rather
than promote, the general welfare and
uphold the safeguards that secure us these
CERTAIN UNALIENABLE RIGHTS …
LIFE, LIBERTY AND THE PURSUIT
OF HAPPINESS.

LET FACTS BE SUBMITTED
TO A CANDID WORLD.

"I think he's done a really great job of outsmarting our country."

Trump on Putin

TKO

A present from Putin was sent

To the Trump team who knew

What that meant

But the press lost its mind

And we were robbed blind

By One-Thousandth of Just 1%.

"If I were to run, I'd run as a Republican.

They're the dumbest voters in the country."

Trump

MEMO FROM THE GOP

"You were so kind to vote us in
You are so very nice
The rich need taxes cut again
From you we'll take a slice."

"But not from us! The middle-class!"
Turning a little blue
"And so un-Christian toward the poor!"
Paul Ryan says, "_____ ____!"

"It seems a shame," some R's now say
To play them such a trick,
After we've brought them to the Right
Now, what if they get sick?"

"Not many of us care, you know
Obamacare is done
The rich will have great healthcare
And you can keep your gun."

"I sorta get away with things like that."

Trump

DEAL

"Dear Pig, are you willing

To sell for one shilling?"

"Sure thing!" said the Piggy, "I will."

So they took it away, the old USA

The Turkeys who live on the Hill.

WHAT COMEY KNEW

Way prior to

The FBI knew

Trump had more than a few

Kremlin ties

"But the emails!" he said

Though the issue was dead

And the polls said she led

(But the margin was slim)

He chose him over her

Instead

Why?

Was a gun to his head?

Were we "better off Red"?

Did someone have something on him?

A "HIGHER" LOYALTY

Some Kind of "loyalty"

To somewhere "above"

Got us this traitor

From Russia with love

Some kind of "loyalty"

To something "higher"

Together with Putin

Got us this liar

BOYCOTT

The Kremlin ties of this White House gang

Was the central plot

We do know how it happened

Now we know a lot

If anyone else is fired

There has to be

A national retail boycott

CRIME'S AT A HIGH

If one child is kidnapped

And we call it a crime

Then what do we call it

The five-hundredth time?

IF ONLY IT HAD BEEN FRANCE

If the Bank of France
Had offered finance
We'd be theirs, and not Russia's, today
Had it been French banks
We'd be telling them thanks
Merci and please have it your way
They would own us, not good, but
It could be okay

Bonjour, bonne chance
To belong to France
A democracy, by the way
Where tax is collected to pay
For healthcare and childcare
Old age care and college
Vive la liberté

Bonjour, bonne chance
To belong to France
A democracy, by the way
Where they take special pains
To get leaders with brains
Vive la égalité

Bonjour, bonne chance
To belong to France
Where the visitors all want to stay
Vive la fraternité
Lafayette, here we come
We'd speak French, at least some
They adore older women, they say

We would smoke and buy clothes
La vie en rose
We'd eat snails
Fall in love every day
Have extended vacations with pay
Moscow is so far away

If only it had been France

ALL ABOUT IMPEACHMENT:
The Safety of The State

"THE PRESIDENT, VICE PRESIDENT AND ALL CIVIL OFFICERS OF THE UNITED STATES SHALL BE REMOVED FROM OFFICE ON IMPEACHMENT FOR, AND CONVICTION OF, TREASON, BRIBERY, OR OTHER HIGH CRIMES AND MISDEMEANORS. " Article III, Section 3, United States Constitution

"TREASON AGAINST THE UNITED STATES, SHALL CONSIST ONLY IN LEVYING WAR AGAINST THEM (those states), *OR, IN ADHERING TO THEIR ENEMIES, GIVING THEM AID AND COMFORT."* Article III, Section 3, United States Constitution

Colonial governors (the first in 1635!), judges, and other royal officials appointed by the king were impeached by the colonists. Rebellion started early.

To the understanding of the colonists, impeachment was a protection against arbitrary power and subverting laws for self-serving ends.

State constitutions included impeachment clauses and were frequently applied to remove judges, governors, and other officials.

For the Founders, high crimes and misdemeanors meant corruption, betrayal of trust to a foreign power for reasons of bribery or some other gain (plain treason), and harm or risk of harm to society.

Whether intentional or not, whether criminal or not, acts having a malign effect on the nation and government were enough to impeach.

The President has three chief responsibilities:

*"(THE PRESIDENT) SHALL TAKE CARE
THAT THE LAWS BE FAITHFULLY
EXECUTED ..."*
Article II, Section 3,
United States Constitution.

*"TO FAITHFULLY EXECUTE THE OFFICE
OF THE PRESIDENT OF THE UNITED
STATES."*
Presidential Oath of Office, Article II,
Section 1, United States Constitution

*"TO PRESERVE, PROTECT, AND DEFEND
THE CONSTITUTION OF
THE UNITED STATES."*
Presidential Oath of Office, Article II,
Section 1, United States Constitution

Betraying the oath of office and endangering the safety of the state are unmistakable high crimes and misdemeanors; grievous and impeachable offenses.

Neglect or violation of presidential duties, whether or not they are criminal offenses, makes him liable to impeachment.

The President himself is accountable for the actions of those he appoints.

Swindling and profiteering officials have been impeached and convicted.

The Founders would have seen dismissal of a Special Counsel empowered to investigate him as just grounds for impeachment. Pardoning himself would be equally grave.

Impeachment was meant to prevent a tyrannical, malfunctioning, feckless or disabled official from retaining power.

The President is not a king.

MERRY BASTILLE DAY

Merry Bastille Day

The President said

Knowing little about it

And to where it led

The words to that old Marseillaise song

He never has read

Hey, was it that l'état c'est moi guy?

Or the après moi le déluge one instead?

Remember what happened the next day

He was quickly cut off from his head

So Merry Bastille Day to you, sir

To you sir, we all tip our hat

Merry Bastille Day to you, sir

You're certainly entitled to that.

PROPOSAL FOR A NEW AMERICAN ELECTION

We the American people demand a new election.
This past election was manipulated and subverted
by Russia, a hostile foreign power. It is therefore
illegitimate. It dishonored our heritage as a free
people.

It is dangerous to say that a truthful investigation
is only necessary "so that it doesn't happen
again," *as if this time doesn't count.*

Is it *safe to wait* and do nothing while
Republican - dominated intelligence committees
finish their work "getting to the bottom of it?"
It has been in plain sight all along.

This was a complete Russian-made coup d'etat,
enabled by many of our elected officials and members
of the press, particularly the networks by providing
unlimited airtime, free of the normal journalistic
examination and hard scrutiny expected in a
democracy.

Trump's preferred policies, anti-NATO, anti-EU, anti-democracy, and anti-American, are identical to Putin's.

The sweeping purge of the State Department and degrading of American power is a *Kremlin dream come true.*

The conspiracy is *self-evident.*
Russia's aggression was designed to help Trump and hurt Clinton and our democratic process.

Putin's plan worked. This fact cannot be ignored.

For almost a year a Russian-generated disinformation operation was waged against the 2016 Democratic presidential candidate, what the Russians call "*Hybrid Warfare.*"

The voters were kept in the dark about the cyber-espionage and the scope of the connections between Trump and the Russians *until after* the election.

The *FBI didn't inform the American public* about the Russian attacks nor did it inform us of Trump's decades long connections to Russian mafia figures. Nearly *everyone* in the Trump campaign had connections to the Kremlin. Instead, ALL focus by the

FBI and the national media was inexplicably on Hillary Clinton's emails.

It appears Comey was instrumental in *sabotaging* her election and allowing a *Russian puppet* and a criminal gang to take power.

It is promoting a myth to say we cannot know how it would have turned out without Putin's sabotage and Comey's as well.

No one can believe these things had *zero* effect. Did they have a tiny effect?

.001% of the total (77,000) from the three swing states IS only a tiny effect.
A TKO, a technical knockout.

A Molotov Cocktail thrown at the Electoral College has shattered our country.

The *real vote*, a margin of victory of almost 3 million, was manifestly the will of the *majority. The consent of the governed.*

Our national sovereignty is being *insulted.* What free country's leaders and press would *surrender* to a *foreign dictator's sabotage* of an election?

It is our right and our duty to throw off such a *foreign*, both *alien* and *seditious*, imposition. This *savage* attack on our norms and values cannot be allowed to continue. *Dismantling of our institutions* must be stopped. There is no recovering what we are losing.

It is our right and our duty to protect our *common wealth, democracy, and lives of our people* from destruction. Russia is not preventing us from having a new fair and free election. But we ourselves are.

With a firm reliance on the guidance of our Founders, *we the majority*, mutually pledge to stop this *train of abuses*.

The Founders never imagined
one party rule and *unfettered gerrymandering*.

The First Amendment of the United States Constitution preserves "the right of the people to petition the government for a redress of grievances."

The power to force this can only come from Democrats *shutting down the government*, as Republicans would have done immediately if a *foreign power tipped* an election in the Democrats' favor. *They would have declared it invalid if foreign interference had been as obvious,* i.e. The Bank of France, etc.

Or it can come from the threat of a *national strike* or *national retail boycott*, which is how it has been done many times before in other countries.

The Founders said, and we say again,

We will stop this despotism encroaching on our sacred democratic inheritance.

We will put an end to this illegitimate, anti-American, openly corrupt and dangerous regime.

December 2016

"I think loyalty to the country, loyalty to the United States is important. It depends on how you define loyalty."

Trump

THE TIME HAS COME, 2018

The Time has come

The Walrus said

To talk of many things

Of coups and Russian sabotage

The gang in the West Wing

So Special Counsel Mueller, dear

What charges will you bring?

Right now we only want to know

How soon will he swing?

THE TIME HAS COME, 2020

It's 2020 now

And things could get much worse

The Spirit of '76

In reverse

In 2020

It's 50-50

Madelynn Gingold is an artist who lives in NYC.
www.madelynngingold.com